OBIT

Also by Victoria Chang

Barbie Chang

The Boss

Salvinia Molesta

Circle

Asian American Poetry: The Next Generation (editor)

Is Mommy? (for children, with Marla Frazee)

Love, Love (for children)

OBIT

VICTORIA CHANG

POEMS

Copper Canyon Press

Port Townsend, Washington

Cover art: Phil Kovacevich

Copper Canyon Press is in residence at Fort Worden State Park
in Port Townsend, Washington, under the auspices of Centrum.
Centrum is a gathering place for artists and creative thinkers from
around the world, students of all ages and backgrounds, and
audiences seeking extraordinary cultural enrichment.

LIBRARY OF CONGRESS CATALOGING-IN-PUBLICATION DATA
Names: Chang, Victoria, 1970– author.
Title: Obit : Poems / Victoria Chang.
Description: Port Townsend, Washington : Copper Canyon Press,
[2020] |
Identifiers: LCCN 2019043837 | ISBN 9781556595745 (trade
paperback)
Subjects: LCSH: Obituaries–Poetry. | LCGFT: Poetry.
Classification: LCC PS3603.H3575 O25 2020 | DDC 811/.6–dc23
LC record available at https://lccn.loc.gov/2019043837

9 8

COPPER CANYON PRESS
Post Office Box 271
Port Townsend, Washington 98368

www.coppercanyonpress.org

For my mother and my children.

Contents

I

II

III

OBIT

I

Give sorrow words; the grief that does not speak

wispers the o'er-fraught heart, and bids it break.

—William Shakespeare, *Macbeth*

My Father's Frontal Lobe—died unpeacefully of a stroke on June 24, 2009 at Scripps Memorial Hospital in San Diego, California. Born January 20, 1940, the frontal lobe enjoyed a good life. The frontal lobe loved being the boss. It tried to talk again but someone put a bag over it. When the frontal lobe died, it sucked in its lips like a window pulled shut. At the funeral for his words, my father wouldn't stop talking and his love passed through me, fell onto the ground that wasn't there. I could hear someone stomping their feet. The body is as confusing as language—was the frontal lobe having a tantrum or dancing? When I took my father's phone away, his words died in the plastic coffin. At the funeral for his words, we argued about my miscarriage. *It's not really a baby,* he said. I ran out of words, stomped out to shake the dead baby awake. I thought of the tech who put the wand down, quietly left the room when she couldn't find the heartbeat. I understood then that darkness is falling without an end. That darkness is not the absorption of color but the absorption of language.

My Mother—died unpeacefully on August 3, 2015 in her room at Walnut Village Assisted Living in Anaheim, California of pulmonary fibrosis. The room was born on July 3, 2012. The Village wasn't really a village. No walnut trees. Just cut flowers. Days before, the hospice nurse silently slid the stethoscope on top of my mother's lung and waited for it to inflate. The way waiting becomes an injury. The way the nurse breathed in, closed his eyes, breathed out, and said *I'm sorry.* Did the blood rush to my face or to my fingertips? Did he reopen his eyes before or after he said *I'm sorry*? The way memory is the ringing after a gunshot. The way we try to remember the gunshot but can't. The way memory gets up after someone has died and starts walking.

Victoria Chang—died unknowingly on June 24, 2009 on the I-405 freeway. Born in the Motor City, it is fitting she died on a freeway. When her mother called about her father's heart attack, she was living an indented life, a swallow that didn't dip. This was not her first death. All her deaths had creases except this one. It didn't matter that her mother was wrong (it was a stroke) but that Victoria Chang had to ask whether she should drive to see the frontal lobe. When her mother said *yes,* Victoria Chang had the feeling of not wanting to. Someone heard that feeling. Because he did not die but all of his words did. At the hospital, Victoria Chang cried when her father no longer made sense. This was before she understood the cruelty of his disease. It would be the last time she cried in front of it. She switched places with her shadow because suffering changes shape and happens secretly.

Victoria Chang—died unwillingly on April 21, 2017 on a cool day in Seal Beach, California, on her way back from the facility named Sunrise, which she often mistakenly called *Sunset.* Her father's problems now her problems, nailed to her frontal lobe. Like a typist, she tried to translate his problems, carry the words back in a pony carriage one by one. When the pony moved, the letters strung together to form sentences. But when the pony refused to move, the carriage disappeared. The letters tagged her and ran into the cornfields. The police came and shined their lights onto the field, started shooting the letters even though they had their hands up. Sometimes, they shot the letters twice, just to make sure. Sometimes, they shot them in the back. When we shoot a letter once, it's called *typing.* Twice, *engraving.* When someone dies, letters are always engraved. When someone dies, there is a constant feeling of wanting to speak to someone, but the plane with all the words is crossing the sky.

Voice Mail—died on June 24, 2009, the voice mail from my father said *Transcription Beta (low confidence)*, *Hello hi um I may be able to find somebody to reduce the size of the car OK I love you.* The Transcription Beta had low self-esteem. It wandered into the river squinting and came back blind. The Transcription Beta could not transcribe dementia. My father really said, *I'll fold the juice*, not *I love you*. Is language the broom or what's being swept? When I first read *I love you*, some hand spun a fine thread around my lungs and tightened. Because my father had never said that to me before. In the seconds before realization of the error, I didn't feel love, but panic. We read to inherit the words, but something is always between us and the words. Until death, when comprehension and disappearance happen simultaneously.

Language—died, brilliant and beautiful on August 1, 2009 at 2:46 p.m. Lover of raising his hand, language lived a full life of questioning. His favorite was twisting what others said. His favorite was to write the world in black and white and then watch people try and read the words in color. Letters used to skim my father's brain before they let go. Now his words are blind. Are pleated. Are the dispatcher, the dispatches, and the receiver. When my mother was dying, I made everyone stand around the bed for what would be the last group photo. Some of us even smiled. Because dying lasts forever until it stops. Someone said, *Take a few.* Someone said, *Say cheese.* Someone said, *Thank you.* Language fails us. In the way that *breaking an arm* means an arm's bone can break but the arm itself can't break off unless sawed or cut. My mother couldn't speak but her eyes were the only ones that were wide open.

Tankas

My children, children,
there's applesauce everywhere
but it's not for you.
It is strange to help someone
grow while helping someone die.

*

Each time I write *hope,*
the letters fray and scatter.
The hopeful poets
never seem to have my dreams,
never seem to have children.

Language—died again on August 3, 2015 at 7:09 a.m. I heard about my mother's difficult nights. I hired a night person. By the time I got there, she was always gone. The night person had a name but was like a ghost who left letters on my lips. *Couldn't breathe, 2:33 a.m. Screaming, 3:30 a.m. Calm, 4:24 a.m.* I got on all fours, tried to pick up the letters like a child at an egg hunt without a basket. But for every letter I picked up, another fell down, as if protesting the oversimplification of my mother's dying. I wanted the night person to write in a language I could understand. *Breathing unfolding, 2:33. Breathing in blades, 3:30. Breathing like an evening gown, 4:24.* But maybe I am wrong, how death is simply death, each slightly different from the next but the final strike all the same. How the skin responds to a wedding dress in the same way it responds to rain.

Victoria Chang—died on June 24, 2011, at the age of 41. Her imagination lived beyond that day though. It weighed two pounds and could be lifted like weights. Once she brought her father to the arcade. He found the basketball machine and shot one after another. As if he were visiting his past self in prison, touching the clear glass at his own likeness. On the other side of the glass, words like *embankment, unsightly,* and *heterogeneous* lived. He tried to ask his former self for help but the guards wouldn't allow him to pass notes. When the ball machine buzzed, he stopped, eyes deformed and wild. He called my dead mother over to see his score, hand waving at me. What happens when the shadow is attached to the wrong object but refuses to let go? I walked over because I wanted to believe him.

The Future—died on June 24, 2009. A pioneering figure in the past, the future was the president of the present. You are sitting. But the future wants your chair. She is demanding. She is not interested in the spine but what it holds up. She is interested in award ceremonies. She is interested in fallen petals that look like medals. She is interested in anything with the word *track* in it, tenure track, deer tracks, tracksuit, but she doesn't want you to get sidetracked or to backtrack. The future can be thrown away by the privileged. But sometimes she just suddenly dies. The way the second person dies when a mother dies, reborn as third person as *my mother.* The way grief is really about future absence. The way the future closes its offices when a mother dies. What's left: a hole in the ground the size of violence.

Civility—died on June 24, 2009, at the age of 68. Murdered by a stroke whose paintings were recently featured in a museum, two square canvases painted white, black scissors in the middle of each, open, pointing at each other. After my father's stroke, my mother no longer spoke in full sentences. Fragments of codfish, the language of savages, each syllable a mechanical dart from her mouth to my father's holes. Maybe this is what happens when language fails, a last breath inward but no breath outward. A state of holding one's breath forever but not dying. When her lungs began their failing, she could still say *you* but not *thank. You don't know what it's like,* she said when I told her to stop yelling at my father. She was right. When language leaves, all you have left is tone, all you have left are smoke signals. I didn't know she was using her own body as wood.

My Mother's Lungs—began their dying sometime in the past. Doctors talked around tombstones. About the hedges near the tombstones, the font. The obituary writer said the obituary is the moment when someone becomes history. What if my mother never told me stories about the war or about her childhood? Does that mean none of it happened? No one sits next to my mother's small rectangular tombstone, flush to the earth. The stone is meant to be read from above. What if I'm in space and can't read it? Does that mean she didn't die? She died at 7:07 a.m. PST. It is three hours earlier in Hawaii. Does that mean in Hawaii she hasn't died yet? But the plane ride to Hawaii is five hours long. This time gap can never be overcome. The difference is called grieving.

Privacy—died on December 4, 2015.
My child brought a balloon that said
Get Well Soon to the gravesite. This
time Peter Manning lay next to my
mother. A stranger so close to her.
Before this other stone appeared, my
mother's stone was still my mother
because of the absence around her.
The appearance of the new stone
and the likeness to her stone implied
my mother was a stone too, that my
mother was buried under the stone
too. On the day of the burial, I hired a
Chinese priest. I couldn't understand
many of his words because they were
not about food. The men who had dug
up the dirt stood with their shovels and
waited. I looked at their eyes for any
sign of drowning. Then I noticed that
one man's body didn't have a shadow.
And when he walked away, the grass
didn't flatten. His shovel was clean. I
suddenly recognized this man as love.

My Mother's Teeth—died twice, once in 1965, all pulled out from gum disease. Once again on August 3, 2015. The fake teeth sit in a box in the garage. When she died, I touched them, smelled them, thought I heard a whimper. I shoved the teeth into my mouth. But having two sets of teeth only made me hungrier. When my mother died, I saw myself in the mirror, her words around my mouth, like powder from a donut. Her last words were in English. She asked for a Sprite. I wonder whether her last thought was in Chinese. I wonder what her last thought was. I used to think that a dead person's words die with them. Now I know that they scatter, looking for meaning to attach to like a scent. My mother used to collect orange blossoms in a small shallow bowl. I pass the tree each spring. I always knew that grief was something I could smell. But I didn't know that it's not actually a noun but a verb. That it moves.

I tell my children
that hope is like a blue skirt,
it can twirl and twirl,
that men like to open it,
take it apart, and wound it.

*

I tell my children
that sometimes I too can hope,
that sometimes nothing
moves but my love for someone,
and the light from the dead star.

Friendships—died June 24, 2009, once beloved but not consistently beloved. The mirror won the battle. I am now imprisoned in the mirror. All my selves spread out like a deck of cards. It's true, the grieving speak a different language. I am separated from my friends by gauze. I will drive myself to my own house for the party. I will make small talk with myself, spill a drink on myself. When it's over, I will drive myself back to my own house. My conversations with other parents about children pass me on the way up the staircase and repeat on the way down. Before my mother's death, I sat anywhere. Now I look for the image of the empty chair near the image of the empty table. An image is a kind of distance. An image of me sits down. Depression is a glove over the heart. Depression is an image of a glove over the image of a heart.

Gait—my father's gait died on March 14, 2011. Once erect, light, flat-footed. Magnificent. Now, his gait shuffles like sandpaper. Once my father erected a basketball net, mounted it onto a wooden pole from the lumberyard to save money. With each shot, the pole moved a little, invisible to the eye, until I had to shoot from the side of the driveway. Now I avoid semicolons. I look for statues whose eyes don't move with me. The kind of people who stand in place and lights can be strung on. The problem is, my father's brain won't stop walking, and my dead mother is everywhere.

Logic—my father's logic died on June 24, 2009 in bright daylight. Murdered in the afternoon. I hung up Missing Person posters of myself and listened for the sound of a tree falling. The sound of the wind through trees is called *psithurism*. There's no word for the translator of wind. If the wind is words, the trees are exclamation points. The spears of moonlight, question marks. My father doesn't realize his words always end in prepositions. *I have a problem with [the moon], there is a problem between [the moon and me], the problem is on [the moon].* What if he can no longer find what is being modified, in the way snow would fall forever if there were no lip to die on.

Optimism—died on August 3, 2015, a slow death into a pavement. At what point does a raindrop accept its falling? The moment the cloud begins to buckle under it or the moment the ground pierces it and breaks its shape? In December, my mother had her helper prepare a Chinese hot-pot feast. My mother said it would probably be her last Christmas. I laughed at her. She yelled at my father all night. I put a fish ball in my mouth. My optimism covered the whole ball as if the fish had never died, had never been gutted and rolled into a humiliating shape. To acknowledge death is to acknowledge that we must take another shape.

Ambition—died on August 3, 2015, a sudden death. I buried ambition in the forest, next to distress. They used to take walks together until ambition pushed distress off the embankment. Now, they put a bracelet around my father's ankle. The alarm rings when he gets too close to the door. His ambitious nature makes him walk to the door a lot. When the alarm rings, he gets distressed. He remembers that he wants to find my house. He thinks he can find my house. His fingerprints have long vanished from my house. Some criminals put their fingers on electric coils of a stove to erase their fingerprints. But it only makes them easier to find. They found my father in the middle of the road last month, still like a bulbless lamp, unable to recall its function, confused like the moon. At the zoo, a great bald eagle sits in a small cage because of a missing wing. Its remaining wing is grief. Above the eagle, a bird flying is the eagle's memory, and its prey, the future.

Chair—my mother's green chair died on August 3, 2015. We arrange chairs in rows facing the same direction to represent reverence. In a circle to represent sharing. Stacked to represent completion. Hanging from the ceiling to represent art. In front of a desk to represent work. Before my mother died, I routed all her mail to my house. Her catalogues still come every day. I imagine her sitting in her chair flipping through them for more shirts that look the same. I understand now, only the living change clothes. Last week, I took my father pants-shopping. I heard him quarreling with the pants. He came out of the dressing room with his pants on backwards. Two pockets facing forward, like my mother's eyes mocking me, as if to say, *I told you so.* He was angry, pointing and cursing at the *chairs* that no longer fit. I entered the men's dressing room and picked up all the pants on the floor because one of them had to be my missing father.

Do you smell my cries?
They come from another place.
The cry comes from you.
Now everything comes from you.
To be empty and so full.

*

I tell my children
that they can wake anything,
that they are not yet
dying. But what do I know?
I know that a mother dies.

Tears—died on August 3, 2016. Once we stopped at a Vons to pick up flowers and pinwheels on our way to the graveyard. It had been a year and death no longer glittered. My ten-year-old putting the flowers perfectly in the small narrow hole in front of the stone. How she somehow knew what the hole was for, that my mother wasn't really on the other side. Suddenly, our sobbing. How many times have I looked into the sky for some kind of message, only to find content but no form. She ran back to the car. The way grief takes many forms, as tears or pinwheels. The way the word *haystack* never conjures up the same image twice. The way we assume all tears taste the same. The way our sadness is plural, but grief is singular.

Memory—died August 3, 2015. The death was not sudden but slowly over a decade. I wonder if, when people die, they hear a bell. Or if they taste something sweet, or if they feel a knife cutting them in half, dragging through the flesh like sheet cake. The caretaker who witnessed my mother's death quit. She holds the memory and images and now they are gone. For the rest of her life, the memories are hers. She said my mother couldn't breathe, then took her last breath twenty seconds later. The way I have imagined a kiss with many men I have never kissed. My memory of my mother's death can't be a memory but is an imagination, each time the wind blows, leaves unfurl a little differently.

Language—died on March 4, 2017. It wanted to live as long as possible in its form, an icicle on the edge of a roof. I lifted the roof off my father's head and found the balcony to stand on. I spoke loudly and slowly about the Guggenheim. Two women at the table across from us with plates of all-you-can-eat snow crab legs, their fourth each. I repeated myself again and again. The women kept getting up for more, their sucking noises like eating an overripe peach. My father finally said that he would like to *see a copy of the pamphlet.* This year they sent a spacecraft on a suicide mission between Saturn and its rings. If I could get between my father and his brain, would I too be committing suicide? If someone is directing the spacecraft, isn't it murder? The pictures sent back are silent. A picture represents a moment that has died. Then every photo is a crime scene. When we remember the dead, at some point, we are remembering the picture, not the moment.

Tomas Tranströmer—died on March 26, 2015, at the age of 83. He wrote: *I am carried in my shadow / like a violin / in its black case. // The only thing I want to say / glitters out of reach / like the silver / in a pawnbroker's.* My father couldn't have written those words before or after his stroke. I wonder if his daughters disliked visiting him as much as I dislike visiting my father. The way his fists stay shut, the way his mind is always out of earshot. The way his words abandon his mouth and each day I pick them up, put them back in, screw the lid on tighter. Sometimes when he complains and no one can understand, I think of all the places I hid as a child. All the times I have silenced someone by covering their mouth with mine.

Approval—died on August 3, 2015 at the age of 44. It died at 7:07 a.m. *How much money will you get* was my mother's response to everything. She used to wrap muffins in a napkin at the buffet and put them in her purse. I never saw the muffins again. What I would do to see those muffins again, the thin moist thread as she pulled the muffin apart. A photo shows my mother holding my hand. I was nine. I never touched her hand again. Until the day before she died. I love so many things I have never touched: the moon, a shiver, my mother's heart. Her fingers felt like rough branches covered with plastic. I trimmed her nails one by one while the morphine kept her asleep. Her nails weren't small moons or golden doors to somewhere, but ten last words I was cutting off.

Sometimes all I have
are words and to write them means
they are no longer
prayers but are now animals.
Other people can hunt them.

*

You don't need a thing
from me, you already have
everything you need:
the moon, a wound on the lake,
our footprints to not follow.

Secrets—died on August 7, 2015 and they were relieved to die. No one at the funeral had known about my mother's illness. No one had known how fiercely my mother and father fought. One Chinese face after another. I told the story. Told it again. Their mouths opened like time. Red sashes with Chinese characters I couldn't read. The stems spoke with their flowers. To look down and see their legs missing. Later, I found a photo of my mother smiling with friends at her home, just the year before. No oxygen tank, no tube in her nose. She must have taken it off, put it in the closet between the beginning of her life and the end of her life. I imagine her panicking inside, waiting for them to leave. The mind and speech assemble and disassemble like geese. Scientists now say that a mind still works after the body has died. That there's a burst of brain energy. Then maybe she heard the geese above disassemble one last time. Then maybe my kiss on her cheek felt like lightning.

Music—died on August 7, 2015. I made a video with old pictures and music for the funeral. I picked "Hallelujah" in a cappella. Because they weren't really singing, but actually crying. When my children came into the room, I pretended I was writing. Instead, I looked at my mother's old photos. The fabric patterns on all her shirts. The way she held her hands together at the front of her body. In each picture, the small brown purse that now sits under my desk. At the funeral, my brother-in-law kept turning the music down. When he wasn't looking, I turned the music up. Because I wanted these people to feel what I felt. When I wasn't looking, he turned it down again. At the end of the day, someone took the monitor and speakers away. But the music was still there. This was my first understanding of grief.

Appetite—died its final death on Father's Day, June 21, 2015, peacefully and quietly among family. We dressed my mother, rolled her down in her wheelchair. The oxygen machine breathing like an animal. They were the only Chinese people at the facility. The center table was loud again, was invite-only again. Like always, I filled my mother's plates with food. Her favorite colored puddings contained in plastic cups. When we got up to leave, her food still there, glistening like worms. No one thought much of it. There are moments that are like brushstrokes, when only much later after the ocean is finished, become the cliff's edge that they were all along. Death is our common ancestor. It doesn't care whom we have dined with.

Appetite—died on March 16, 2015.
Once, in graduate school, I was
the only one to order a drink at the
restaurant. My boyfriend did not like
this. He dropped me off in the middle
of town to walk home. I looked at
the children's clothing in the window,
the little striped cap, pink dress, and
thought about beauty. I spun around
to avoid darkness but darkness was
the one spinning me. I hid in a bright
Taco Bell. The man at the register
had a narrow hole for a mouth and a
brown mass on his cheek. He was
so beautiful that I thought he must be
Death. Twenty years later, my mother
requested Taco Bell for lunch. I ran out
to buy her bags and bags of tacos. No
one in line understood my emergency.
The man I handed my credit card to
had a brown mass on his face. He
nodded when he handed me the bag,
as if he knew. My mother pressed her
lips to the tacos, as if she were kissing
someone for the rapturous last time.

Form—died on August 3, 2015. My children sleep with framed photos of my mother. Leaden, angular, metal frames. My ten-year-old puts her frame in the red velvet bag that held the cremation urn and brings it with her on vacation. A photo of my mother sits in the bag that once held a container of her ashes. When we die, we are represented by representations of representations, often in different forms. Memories too are representations of the dead. I go through corridors looking for the original but can't find her. In Palm Springs, the desert fails me. Dust, sand, gravel, bits of dead things everywhere, a speck of someone else's dead mother blows into my eye and I start crying again. The heat is now too optimistic. The pool and its luster like an inquisition. My own breathing, between the splashes and children laughing, no longer a miracle, but simple mathematics.

Optimism—died on August 3, 2015,
of monotony. Before my sister would
fly home, she and my mother would
cry together. The one time my mother
cried to me, I said, *The doctor's wrong,*
you don't know how long—it could be
a year or more. She didn't stop crying.
I got up and left the room. Outside,
three floors below, behind the building,
a family was celebrating something
in their yard. Piñatas, music, children
momentarily suspended above Earth
in a bounce house. That summer,
we were not on Earth, but pacing in
a building above it. People in a city
can spend a lifetime never actually
touching the earth once. I was so
afraid their happiness would rise up
through the window like steam. I could
hear the thumping of the sticks on
the piñata, once a happy anticipation,
altered to the inevitability of the candy
dropping. Now I close my eyes and
try to remember the optimism of the
thumping, the origin of things.

I can't say with faith
that I would run toward a bus
to save you from death.
If a girl is only as
good as her mother, then what?

*

To love anyone
means to admit extinction.
I tell myself this
so I never fall in love,
so that the fire lights just me.

Hands—died on January 13, 2015. My mother's handwriting had become jagged and shaky. Bodies jump out of bed. Feet leap off of bridges. Hands never leap. They flag people down. They gesture to enhance language. They are the last part of hugging, which the body mostly does. They wipe off the tears that the eyes release. They write on paper the things the brain sends. After my mother died, I looked at a photo where she had moved into assisted living from the ER. Her oxygen tube in her nose, my two small children standing on each side. Her hands around their hands pulled tightly to her chest, the chorus of knuckles still housed, white stones, soon to be freed, soon to be splashing.

Oxygen—died on March 12, 2012. At first, it came in heavy green canisters. Then a large rolling machine that pushed air day and night. When my mother changed her clothes, she had to take the tube out of her nose. She stopped to catch her breath, as if breath were constantly in motion, as if it could be chased. I'm not sure when I began to notice her panic without the oxygen, in the way we don't notice a leaf turning red or an empire falling. One day, it just appears, as if it had been there all along. Like the hospice staff with their papers, bags of medicine, their garlands of silence. Like grief, the way it dangles from everything like earrings. The way grief needs oxygen. The way every once in a while, it catches the light and starts smoking. The way my grief will die with me. The way it will cleave and grow like antlers.

Reason—died on June 24, 2009, like make-believe trees that just get taken down and put away. My father's words taken out of his brain and left downstairs. Remote but close, like a wound on your child or a curtain blowing in the other room. This week, he is obsessed with the scheduled walks again. This week he doesn't want to wait for the other much older but sharper residents. The memory of reason is there, of once pulling the ropes. When reason dies, determination does not. As in, my father is determined to walk at 10 a.m. at a certain pace. As in his body is determined to move forward with or without his brain, which is two empty slippers nailed into the ground.

Home—died on January 12, 2013. The first of five moves meant the boxes were still optimistic that they would be opened. They were still stiff, arrogant about their new shape, flatness just a memory. At the new house, my father on one of his obsessive walks found the one old Chinese person, a bony lady with branches for teeth, the kind of woman my mother would normally shun because of her background. She visited my mother every day for a year. She brought oranges, vegetables, a salesperson from a funeral home. My father left them to speak in Chinese as he wandered the neighborhood so he wouldn't die. The lady swore at my father in Chinese. Called him *stupid*. A *fool*. At the funeral, she said, *God brought me here to help your mother.* And it struck me. My father's words were an umbrella that couldn't open. My mother held the umbrella, refused to let the wind take it. And this old woman was the wind.

Memory—died on July 11, 2015. When I returned from a trip, my mother on the edge of the bed, hair mostly white, black dye underneath, like a memory. Sheets off the bed in a corner like crushed birds. The caretaker hadn't come for a week. My father pacing, his hands tried to speak for him. Too much pressure on the hands. No one knew what happened that week but the hands. My mother had soiled herself. It was all over her hair that she had rolled in pink curlers one by one her whole life. She denied the soiling. Yelled at me in Chinese for saying it. My child and I bathed her as she sat on the shower chair, naked, slumped over, a defeated animal. Death was still abstract, it could slip down the drain. Sadness was still indivisible. In twenty-three days, it would detonate and shower us like confetti. The water flattened my mother's hair and began burying her tongue.

II

Let the stars
Plummet to their dark address,

Let the mercuric
Atoms that cripple drip
Into the terrible well,

You are the one
Solid the spaces lean on, envious.
You are the baby in the barn.

—Sylvia Plath, from "Nick and the Candlestick"

I Am a Miner. The Light Burns Blue.

A herd of   ribs   ripped   the   eggs

out   of   us   what's left   thousands

of wingless bees   that shake in place   that no

longer make   goods   that no longer   think

clearly   drunk stripes   collide   figures on the TV

rub like   driftwood   babies' heads   turn

toward them   shapes that have   separated   from

their   bodies   everything   is drifting   the frames

of the houses   are missing   what's left drapes   like a

shirt   mothers sit underneath and   sew water   here

the pages are   turning but no one is   reading   here

we are   not talented   here we are   torrential and

babies are always growing   here one light   in one

house on   one street beats on   in   pain

*

If they say that   happiness is   water   that it

is always   growing   then my kind   must be the

lunar crater kind   circular in its shape stingy in its   flow

sometimes I cannot   control its   shedding its   rebellion

other times   it flash freezes and I chip   away   with an

ice pick until my   fingers   freeze into an   artichoke a man with a stroller says   it's worth it   but   it feels

like   hooves on my face   I   cannot   bench-press it

I want a   fixed income of you   so   I can tell you   I don't

want   you to stay   I want   to wake each

morning and find   your   cloth figure next   to me

I want   to prick you and   paw   you   I want to

be   your inseam   to   tailor you   to   wear

you   to   be   you

*

If you are   the portobello   we are the   undersides

of   portobellos   the keyed-in lips ·   even

desire is   split   stained glass   divides

our faces   into   abundance   each day we

are   redivided   each day   we try to push our

selves   back together   like grass   each day   the night

detonates   tries to stick   itself to   morning   light

each day   we are   renamed like a   new   monsoon

we are sculled again   and   again as   saline is

hit by drips   each   strike   different   from

the next   here   we are   sick but   have no

symptoms   here the   rain   is always crowded

here we   always   wear   gowns with

open backs but   don't know   why

*

An old man   pushes up   a clavicle of a lime tree

only the   ashes know why   they   fall from his

cigarette like   asterisks   he doesn't look up   our bodies

and   strollers overlap   fresh cement steams   against

stucco homes and   new sod   babies' faces   reflect on

storefronts   our skin   like   cactuses   we are

latched to   this   landscape   where trees   need

wooden sticks to   stand   straight   where workers trim

thistles   on the trail   each day working   their way

west   and   back   where fields are   aerated into

Chinese checker boards   plugs of   brown dirt strewn

like   confetti like something to   celebrate   where

we try to shed   ruin   at daylight but   by   nightfall

our   hands are always wilderness

*

I am a clubfoot   twisted in   inverted   down I am

the   one in every   one thousand   sandstorm a man

said you should be   happy look at the   child you

have   but if happiness   is   within the   child

then happiness   runs   away   up the   ladder

through the blue   tunnel   down the   slide

I want   straightness   unbending   I chase my
other foot like   a lottery   I search to be the one-in-
ten-million winner   power to my powerball   my mega
of millions   my factorial   capability   factoring in
the wind   the windows   and the probability of   rain
what's left in my winnings   is always this   I want to go
home now   I want my own   room forever   I want
what I used   to have   I want   what I have

*

In the last parking lot   in the last city   there are
trees that   look   like   nerve endings   scalps of   leaves
thousands of birds in   threes   somewhere   the
last people   have   stopped   to   place   white rocks over
dried volcano   Beth loves   Jim and   someone loves
Matt   at the last party   the   light   lanced onto
the last baby's   face   its body still   slumping   in
ignorance   once while teaching a   child how   to draw
a person   I learned we are made   only of circles and
rectangles   I now know   a body must   loosen before
it tightens   I now know a body   can loosen   and
tighten with   many men   I now know   Earth   is a
hole   not a   sphere   meant   to   be   filled
with   bodies   not with   thinking

50

*

Circular saws   grinding gristle   tightening time

I wonder whether   time is running   away from

death   or toward death   I   wonder   whether

death   sounds this   way or whether death   has

no sound   the food truck   blows   its horn   the

sun pushes   and   pushes   nine   mothers with

strollers   babies sit upright like kites   the statue of

a woman has   a space   where the   heart should be

through the space   on the other side of   the park   is

an American flag   a man must have   made   this statue

we are always looking   through   women   the men

are nearly done building   the wall   stone   by

stone   we have   wiped drops of milk   off   of

lips   and   entertained   the   treetops

*

Yesterday I had my   own room with   my own

milkweed but I didn't   want   to be   there

downstairs a baby rolled   across the floor for

the first time   like dawn   she laughed   clapped

then cried as she   rolled into   the couch   in gaining

control she   loses control   I dreamed   that I

could finally   leave the house   but I had to

travel through   an alley of bees   the alley was

six feet wide   · the bees were six inches   long   they

buzzed in   my spine   led me north led me to a town

where everyone worked near   apple trees   where no one

made flags   where   everyone learned how to multiply

silence how to divide   sadness into small   parcels

how to   gather   colors and give them   away

*

Everyone wanted   poems   with an emperor a head

looped inside a rope   but this   poem is   tepid   this

poem is no epic   the trail the   hedge   a man on a

tractor digging   divots out of a   field   as if   the

field is   just a field   and not   flesh   one   by

one   the bugs like small   beans lift   out of   the

grass   there is   no other way   thousands

of them   they recede   into balls when   kicked

worm bodies that   roll like earth   they are voiceless

but we cannot   extinguish their screams a grotesque

story but not a   big story   there is   war even here

there is a metal machine   there is   a senseless   task

there is terror   our   disregard and billions of

bodies rushing   out   like smoked   bees

*

We are disregarding   planets again   Pluto is no

longer one they say   in a show of hands   where

are   the bodies if   all the hands   go on deck   when

the hands return how   do they find   their bodies

all around the   earth   people spend   one year

chanting   hands hands   fingers thumbs dum ditty

dum ditty   dum dum dum   unlike sharks   we

do not hunt   by   hearing each   other's   hearts

we hunt   with our   hands   how our   hands are

always   behind   a wheel on a road   that divides

pines   into   tribes   on Saturday   someone's

hand will   tighten the   noose   around   another

man's neck   we   will write   about it with   our hands

that   can't however they   try remain housed   like a   heart

*

The rain is   undressed   from the sky   the soil

opens   takes   rain in   as if   it has   the

answers   because the soil   has no   choice

because   the soil is   assaulted too   there   are

diamonds   deep in   the   forest of   soil

pustules   of   God   if you heat a   diamond at

high temperatures   it   will   dissolve   into thin
air like   a   woman   there are   diamonds
beneath a   baby's foot and   its soft nail   clippings
here   the rain does   not have   a mouth   it is
more slap   than tongue   congrats the cards say
hand wash me   your   little mouth   says
as   it   kisses   me   the raindrops   reflect
my face   into   millions   of   yous

*

If darkness   could be   combed there would be
hundreds of   knots   morning and   night
cross   on the   concrete   a snail   flattened
into the   shape of a   scream   a fish has   broken
from the   water   its   rod of a body   flickers on
the dirt   walkers   cross   over   its   eye
somewhere   a child   tries to   wake   up   by
thrashing its   body   somewhere bugs grip   thugs
of dirt   and the worms   look more   beautiful
dead   a bee   catches on a   stroller's wheel and
crackles   as if   its heart can   be   broken   if we
push   the wheel   forward   we   ignore   death if
we walk backwards   we repeat   death   so we
stand   still   and try to   outlast   death

*

Two life-sized tarp   snowmen   held   still by

strings   bleeding light on a lawn   deer   with

moving heads and   little bulbs   look   at him

climbing   up   and down the ladder   a ladder that

begins and ends   differently the bottom   can

hear   the worms coming   out   of   the soil

the top sees   the dust on the   underside of a

moon   it is both dust and   a metaphor   for

marriage   I hate the lawn   the snowmen   the

carrot nose the   queasy smile   the end of   nature but

I know nothing   the baby sees   the glow the

snowmen and   laughs   how can I explain Easter then

we paint the eggs   we hide the eggs   we find the eggs

we put salt on   them   and we   eat   them

*

A spider works each   day   not to   make   beauty

but to eat   how the human mind is   detached

from the heart at   the perfect   distance   the distance

is how   we don't see   everything as   beauty

the difference   between   the spider   and   us is   we

can   let things live   For Sale signs on lawns   shadows rising but   sinking   once we pass   summer   has

wounded   the empty   beef jerky bag   erased

half of   someone's list   near the gutter   what's

left   *brown*   *umber*   *cottage*   the mystery   is

how   the list seems   placed with   such

care   as one   might prop   a batch of lilacs

against   the roadside   and how   we   know

the flowers   don't   represent   beauty

*

I am   thinking   about happiness again   how

you are in some   alternate orthography   perhaps you

are the   raised bumps in braille   perhaps your presence

allows   me to   examine the low   pressure area

the part that often   brings rain   without the clapping

and the   murmurs that   are you   how would I   see an

echo   as   anything   other than grieving   light is here but

it is a   complement   what is the sun but   a source of

light and   what is   light   but a wavelength   detectable by

the eye   light is not   happiness   I seek the underside

of you   the mossy   dark follicle side   light includes

everything   it is perfectly   bound   and because perfect

darkness is   impossible   to create   I seek it as an eye

seeks the   black   cavity of   another eye

*

Another   morning   finally   a man is   hired to

drag   a metal grid over   a dirt path as if   dirt   too

needs   to be   tamed   another man is   speed

walking   arms   beating   the photo on   his

lanyard faded   his eyes in a truce   a woman so thin

she has no   face   blank from running   marathons

her   body remembers   pain in a   different way   than

it remembers   suffering   pain is a   sail on a boat

suffering are many distant sails   she   passes   a   baby in

a stroller   reaching for his   toes   he is practicing   how

to grab   a   girl   how far can   a girl   run

into   the woods   a girl   can   run   halfway

into   the woods   from then on   she is   trying

to run   out   of   the woods

*

If a man is   earth   then a woman is   a beaker

that   sits on   earth   on a stack of   other

beakers in a   cabinet   in a school   if a

woman   is a   beaker   then a   baby is a   watch

glass   that covers   her evenly   that   doesn't

completely   seal her so   gases can still   exchange

57

if a baby is a   watch glass   then   poetry is

the   moon   that tries to   slope   its light

through   the   watch glass   into   an   undividable

glare   graduating down the side   like a   tassel

up over   the watch glass   leaving   drops

that   bloom   like   frost on a   shrub

expanding   everything   underneath .   in

white   blaze

*

The end of   running   of ambition is   a loaf of

hard   white   bread   unbladed on   a wooden table

I still want to cut   the bread   to eat the bread but

it's   too late   I still want to   shake the   saltshaker

pregnant in the shape of a   snowman   the disfigured

the hardened the simple   the snowman's eyes are not   a

window   they are stillborn as   paper   here there are   no

Greek gods   just   the spiky cries of a   baby and the

private legend of   her birth   here   success is not having

a wax figure made   of you   its mucus spit   skin flakes

kisses turn to   rashes   rashes ruffle around   wrists

in the end of   ambition there is   snow   shaped   like

faith   dice   to   give   away   the end of   everything

masculine   and vials   and vials   of   joy

58

III

For last year's words belong to last year's language
And next year's words await another voice.

−T.S. Eliot, *Four Quartets*

Friendships—died a slow death after August 3, 2015. The friends visited my father. They sat in chairs and spoke Chinese. Wore dictionaries for coats. Strange looks between spouses. The friends went home feeling good that they had done their duty, picked up odds and ends of words. Each had memories of offices, of seeing the other side of the sun. The visits lessened and lessened. They were being pursued by their own deaths. I wonder about the leaves and their relationship with fruit. Do the leaves care about the swelling of the fruit? Does the fruit consider the leaves while it expands? Maybe the leaves shade the fruit as it grows and the fruit emits fragrance for the leaves. But eventually, each must face its own falling alone.

Caretakers—died in 2009, 2010, 2011, 2012, 2013, 2014, 2015, 2016, 2017, one after another. One didn't show up because her husband was arrested. Most others watched the clock. Time breaks for the living eventually and we can walk out of doors. The handle of time's door is hot for the dying. What use is a door if you can't exit? A door that can't be opened is called a wall. On the other side, glass can bloom. My father is on the other side of the wall. Tomatoes are ripening on the other side. I can see them through the window that also can't be opened. A window that can't be opened is just a see-through wall. Sometimes we're on the inside as on a plane. Most of the time, we're on the outside looking in such as doggie day care. I don't know if the tomatoes are the new form of his language or if they're simply for eating. I can't ask him because on the other side, there are no words. All I can do is stare at the nameless bursting tomatoes and know they have to be enough.

Subject Matter—always dies, what we are left with is architecture, form, sound, all in a room, darkened, a few chairs unarranged. The door is locked from the inside. But still, subject matter breaks in and all the others rise. My mother's death is not her story. My father's stroke is not his story. I am not my mother's story, not my father's story. But there is a meeting place that is hidden, one that holds all the maps toward indifference. Can pain be separated from subject matter? Can subject matter take flight and lose its way, peck on another tree? How do you walk heavily with subject matter on your back, without trampling all the meadows?

Sadness—dies while the man across the street trims the hedges and I can see my children doing cartwheels. Or in the moment I sit quietly and listen to the sky, consider the helicopter or the child's hoarse breathing at night. Time after a death changes shape, it rolls slightly downhill as if it knows to move itself forward without our help. Because after a death, there is no *moving on* despite the people waving us through the broken lights. There is only a stone key that fits into one stone lock. But the dead are holding the key. And the stone is a boulder in a stream. I wave my memories in, beat them with a wooden spoon, just for a moment, to stop the senselessness of time, the merriment, just for a moment to feel the tinsel of death again, its dirty bloody beak.

Empathy—died sometime before January 20, 2017. The gate vanished but we don't know when. The doorbell vanished. The trains stopped moving. Someone stole the North Pole sign. I am you, and you, and you. But there are so many obstacles between us. I can never feel my mother's illness or my father's dementia. The black notes on the score are only representations of sound, the keys must knock certain strings which are made of steel, steel is made of iron and carbon from the earth. Why do we make things like a piano that try to represent beauty or pain? Why must we always draw what we see? *Just copy it,* my mother used to say about drawing. The artist is only visiting pain, imagining it. We praise the artist, not the apple, not the apple's shadow which is murdered slowly. There must be some way of drawing a picture so that it doesn't become an elegy.

The Obituary Writer—can die before the subject. John Wilson died in 2002, before the publication of his obituary on bandleader Artie Shaw who died in 2004. What if I die before my father? I've written his obituary in my head every day since his stroke. My father's brain has died before him. It was surrounded by his beloved skull. What if the hinges on his skull break and the brain falls out? Do I give it back or toss it? What if we call the waiter over and God comes instead? Do we offer Him a seat and a brandy or do we cover our eyes and hope He doesn't see us? My mother spent years knowing she would die. But in her last days, she had no idea. To suffer for so long with knowledge but not to finish what was known. Why do I need her to know in her last moments? Like the people who died in the Oakland warehouse fire, crawling on the floor, trying to sort between a battered organ and a door, between a staircase and a shadow. Death isn't the enemy. Knowledge of death is the enemy.

Do you see the tree?
Its secrets grow as lemons.
Sometimes I pretend
I love my children more than
words—no one knows this but words.

*

My children, children,
today my hands are dreaming
as they touch your hair.
Your hair turns into winter.
When I die, your hair will snow.

The Doctors—died on August 3, 2015, surrounded by all the doctors before them and their eyes that should have been red but weren't. The Russian doctor knew death was near before anyone else, first said the word *hospice,* a word that looks like *hospital* and *spice.* Which is it? To yearn for someone's quick death seems wrong. To go to the hospital cafeteria and hunch over a table of toast, pots of jam, butter glistening seems wrong. To want to extend someone's life who is suffering seems wrong. Do we want the orchid or the swan swimming in the middle of the lake? We can touch the orchid and it doesn't move. The orchid is our understanding of death. But the swan is death.

Yesterday—died at midnight. All gold. Wet handkerchiefs from mourning. John Updike once said, *Each day, we wake slightly altered, and the person we were yesterday is dead. So why, one could say, be afraid of death, when death comes all the time?* Updike must not have watched someone slowly suffocating. Our air goes in and out like silk in the folders of the lungs. But breathing is a lucky accident. Updike must not have seen Death bring glasses of water but not speak. He must have never carried time over his shoulders as it bled. I think he would change his mind, now having gone through death. His words might no longer come out as birds, but as bandages. The living seem to be the only ones who hypothesize about death. The only ones who try to lift it up.

Grief—as I knew it, died many times. It died trying to reunite with other lesser deaths. Each morning I lay out my children's clothing to cover their grief. The grief remains but is changed by what it is covered with. A picture of oblivion is not the same as oblivion. My grief is not the same as my pain. My mother was a mathematician so I tried to calculate my grief. My father was an engineer so I tried to build a box around my grief, along with a small wooden bed that grief could lie down on. The texts kept interrupting my grief, forcing me to speak about nothing. If you cut out a rectangle of a perfectly blue sky, no clouds, no wind, no birds, frame it with a blue frame, place it faceup on the floor of an empty museum with an open atrium to the sky, that is grief.

Doctors—died on July 16, 2014. Dr. Lynch was supposed to be the best. I researched. I called. I asked. I read. All my schooling had prepared me to help my mother. I was the youngest and most educated child of Death. A hundred people in the waiting room all pulling green oxygen cylinders. I had all the air to myself but I couldn't breathe. We waited two hours. The doctor wore a blue banker shirt, silky red tie that covered his lungs. My mother pointed at me, *I want to live longer so I can spend more time with her.* I think she meant my children, what I represented. The doctor clipped the X-rays to the little box of light. His pen pointed to all the extra dark spots. I was supposed to feel something as he spoke. I looked away because I've never looked at the insides of my mother before. The seeing was the wrong way. I know now that to be loved as a child means to be watched. In high school, I loved when the teacher turned the lights off. A moment to feel loved and unseen at once. I understand now. We can't be loved when the lights are off.

Blame—wants to die but cannot. Its hair is untidy but it's always here. My mother blamed my father. I blamed my father's dementia. My father blamed my mother's lack of exercise. My father is the story, not the storyteller. I eventually blamed my father because the story kept on trying to become the storyteller. Blame has no face. I have walked on its staircase around and around, trying to slap its face but only hitting my own cheeks. When some people suffer, they want to tell everyone about their suffering. When the brush hits a knot, the child cries out loud, makes a noise that is an expression of pain but not the pain itself. I can't feel the child's pain but some echo of her pain, based on my imagination. Blame is just an echo of pain, a veil across the face of the one you blame. I blame God. I want to complain to the boss of God about God. What if the boss of God is rain and the only way to speak to rain is to open your mouth to the sky and drown?

Time—died on August 3, 2015. A week before my mother died, the nurse called and said to *be prepared.* I looked through my purse for the rest of the words. My pockets empty. Prepared for what? Could I prepare if the words were missing? Is a stem with a bud considered a flower? A bud is not a flower but a soon-to-be flower. No word exists for *about to die* but *dying* but even dying lacks time in the same way a bud lacks a timeline. My mother thought it was only an infection. She blamed them for not giving her antibiotics sooner. But time was ahead of her, the wheel already turning. The nurse said after, *I'm surprised she made it through the weekend.* I was surprised she died at all. Time isn't a moment. Time is enlarged, blurry. As in, my ten-year-old wrapped my dead mother's bracelet for her own birthday and said it was a gift.

Today I show you
the people living in tents.
If you lean in and
listen, the lemon makes noise,
pound your fist and it will fall.

*

My children, children,
do you know a dead heart chimes?
That my breath is an
image that you will forget,
you will lift it like a sheet.

Form—died on August 3, 2015. After my mother died, the weather got hotter so gradually we all became blind. Another bird fell out of the ficus, left its eggs. The arm that turned the earth never bothered to stop for the bird and the bird was crushed between the earth and time. After my mother died, my love for her lost all shape. Everything I had disliked about her became fibrous. I let them harden and suffocate. I posted about her last days on an online pulmonary fibrosis board, typing to strangers into the night, the edges of our fingertips touching. That story is still there but I can no longer find it or the people who might be dead. Each letter a small soldier in formation for a new dying person to read, to see how the living might perceive them when they are unconscious. Grief isn't what spills out of a cracked egg. Grief is the row of eggs waiting in the cold to lose their shape.

Control—died on August 3, 2015, along with my mother. Suddenly I was no longer in the middle of the earth. Suddenly I could change the angle of the liquid pen so that the rocket went the other way. And all the children stopped crying. My sister set up the appointment with the neurologist who asked, *What's your name?* My father said, *What what the system is… what,* as he reached into his wallet and gave the doctor his credit card. His finger angrily pointing at me. We left with prescriptions for my father—antidepressants, antianxiety, anger-management pills. My mother hadn't thought to medicate him. So much depends on the questions we ask. *How is he feeling* versus *how are you feeling* is the difference between life and death. I held on to the small white paper as it waved slowly in the wind like a surrender flag. That day dusk didn't arrive. I went into it.

The Situation—died on August 3, 2015, at least part of the situation; my father was the other situation. A situation isn't like a jacket you can just take off the person. The situation is the skin, the body's eggshell, its flowerpot. If you pull the arms off a clock, you still have the clock. Time keeps going because the arms measure time but are not time. To want the situation to die but not the person is like wanting the gallop but not the horse. There are many things I can't put into a box: wind, marvel, time, suffering. I have no answer. I have no more questions. Because *when?* means the situation will be over. My face will carry those of two dead people. And I can finally put down the dictionary.

Memory—died on February 12, 2015. It was a routine. We'd arrive, the children would give my mother a hug, leave the room to watch TV, and I would sit on a small stool ten feet away from the La-Z-Boy chair I had given her. The oxygen machine tired and gurgling, my father pacing in the other room. *Alibaba,* my mother said. *What?* I asked. *Alibaba,* she repeated, *I should buy some.* Again and again she asked me over several weeks as if for the first time. I can still hear her voice, the shrill accented chorus of the *A,* the *li,* then *baba,* the same phrase for father in Chinese. Even as she was dying, she thought the path to God was money. I wonder if she heard coins in her dreams, if when God touched her forehead, His fingertips felt like gold. I bought her the Alibaba shares in March, and it's up 40.64%.

Doctors—died on August 3, 2015. Dr. Lynch, Dr. Chang, Dr. Mahoney, the ER doctors, the nurses, their blank faces as they pulled thin blankets up to my mother's shoulders, the frozen summers. When Dr. Mahoney finally arrived, I forgot all my questions. My heart opened like a tear. He said he was leaving the practice and I wondered why we call groups of doctors a *practice,* as if not yet experts. Maybe because they can't know how to die until they die. When he spoke, I tried not to emit warmth. He wanted to *do something different,* as if saving my mother could be a career option. He talked for twenty minutes. We forgot about my mother in the small bed, just a curtain separating her and the three moaning women. How we go in and out of caring about others. As I returned to my mother's room, I slid down the microscope and felt myself shrinking.

Obsession—born on January 20, 1940, never died after the stroke but grew instead. The stroke gained an oak door, not just hard but impenetrable. The obsessions lived in solitude behind the oak door. After his stroke, the obsession took my father to the gym to walk on the treadmill. He walked as if through a wildfire, he walked so much, he disappeared. His brain now had an accent and no one could understand how to stop him from learning the new language. My mother called and said he fell on the treadmill, hit his head, blood thinners spread his blood like moonlight. They drilled holes in his head, vacuumed out the blood and more words. My father was finally arrested, he turned in the rest of his words, they bound his tongue. And he dreamed in blank paper.

My children, children,
tonight, during a reading,
a white writer said:
She was a squinty-eyed cunt.
My *squinty eyes* remain closed.

*

My children don't have
squinty eyes, they have breathing.
Their breathing sends roads
into the white man's body.
These roads can lead to starlings.

The Clock—died on June 24, 2009 and it was untimely. How many times my father has failed the *clock test.* Once I heard a scientist with Alzheimer's on the radio, trying to figure out why he could no longer draw a clock. It had to do with the *superposition of three types.* The hours represented by 1 to 12, the minutes where a 1 no longer represents 1 but 5, and a 2 now represents 10, then the second hand that measures 1 to 60. I sat at the stoplight and thought of the clock, its perfect circle and its *superpositions,* all the layers of complication on a plane of thought, yet the healthy read the clock in one single instant without a second thought. I think about my father and his lack of first thoughts, how every thought is a second or third or fourth thought, unable to locate the first most important thought. I wonder about the man on the radio and how far his brain has degenerated since. Marvel at how far our brains allow language to wander without looking back but knowing where the pier is. If you unfold an origami swan, and flatten the paper, is the paper sad because it has seen the shape of the swan or does it aspire toward flatness, a life without creases? My father is the paper. He remembers the swan but can't name it. He no longer knows the paper swan represents an animal swan. His brain is the water the animal swan once swam in, holds everything, but when thawed, all the fish disappear. Most of the words we say have something to do with fish. And when they're gone, they're gone.

Hope—died on October 15, 2014 when the FDA approved two drugs, Esbriet and Ofev for pulmonary fibrosis. I did what I was trained to do, researched, read, asked questions. I taped to my wall articles that now look like tombstones. Hope is the wildest bird, the one that flies so fast it will either disappear or burst into flames. My mug from Japan says *Enjoy the Happiness Time.* As if it knows happiness is attached to time somehow. The drugs could slow down the disease but not reverse it. We chose hospice. In my child's homework: *Which of the following happens eventually?* *a) You are born, b) You die, c) A long winter comes to an end, d) Practice makes perfect.* I no longer know how to answer this.

The Head—died on August 3, 2015. When the two men finally came, they rolled a gurney into the other room, hushed talking and noises, then the tip of the gurney came out like a cruise ship. They were worried about dinging the walls. My mother's whole body covered with a blanket. Her head gone. Her face gone. Rilke was wrong. The body is nothing without the head. My mother, now covered, was no longer my mother. A covered apple is no longer an apple. A sketch of a person isn't the person. Somewhere, in the morning, my mother had become the sketch. And I would spend the rest of my life trying to shade her back in.

The Blue Dress—died on August 6, 2015, along with the little blue flowers, all silent. Once the petals looked up. Now small pieces of dust. I wonder whether they burned the dress or just the body? I wonder who lifted her up into the fire? I wonder if her hair brushed his cheek before it grew into a bonfire? I wonder what sound the body made as it burned? They dyed her hair for the funeral, too black. She looked like a comic character. I waited for the next comic panel, to see the speech bubble and what she might say. But her words never came and we were left with the stillness of blown glass. The irreversibility of rain. And millions of little blue flowers. Imagination is having to live in a dead person's future. Grief is wearing a dead person's dress forever.

Hindsight—never existed until August 3, 2015. Someone had painted over hindsight. But if you paint over something, it still exists. On some nights, while the children brush their teeth, I hide under their blankets and jump out when they return. I try to make myself as flat as possible, try not to move as if I have died. Every time, I run out of air. Every time, I realize I don't want to die. Every time, I realize death doesn't care what I want. Sometimes, a child screams, but most of the time, they see my shape or my foot and know I am alive. I wish I had known exactly when my mother would die. As in an appointment. Then I would have moved my feelings earlier. I wouldn't have painted over her mouth. I wouldn't have painted over my heart. Now that it's over, I know the heart doesn't really shatter, but I also can no longer feel it.

The Priest—died on August 3, 2015.
As he died, he cursed. When the
priest first started coming, he left
a watermark on the door. As time
passed, my mother's door was riddled
with bullets from his fist. He started
sending me prayers with his eyes. I
didn't want his prayers. I had too many
selves for God to save. None of my
selves knew how to say sorry. None of
my selves knew each other. I wonder
if my mother took God in toward
the end? The way she had once
cared for her fifty bonsai plants each
morning, snipping gently, adjusting tiny
sprinklers, beckoning them with her
breath. The bonsai barely responded,
had never asked to be limited. She
said the priest was *weird,* would look
at her in a creepy way. As if he knew
she was not a believer but a refugee.
When she arrived in this country, they
painted over her skin. Her fungal toes
only looked like roots.

I put on a shirt,
put on a pair of work pants
because I will die.
How the snow falls to its death,
how snow is just dressed-up rain.

*

Where do they find hope?
Sometimes the city has pleats,
sometimes the body
rings with joy shaped like violets,
sometimes the night wind tingles.

The Car—it was difficult work to take away. It died on March 13, 2015. Before my mother died, my father studied for six months for the DMV test, as if it were an entrance exam to heaven. My mother found him old tests in Chinese. He sat at the table, hand to his head, mumbling, walking so many times to my mother's chair a small river formed under him. *2. God suddenly cuts in front of you creating a hazard. Which of these actions should you take first? a) Honk and step on the brake firmly, b) Take your foot off the gas, c) Swerve into the lane next to you. Is there a choice d? Accelerate and run God over.*

My Mother's Favorite Potted Tree—
died in 2016, a slow death. The day
I looked up, the pink blossoms gone,
the branches shabby opium pipes.
The pot the only thing recognizable.
I had moved the tree here and it had
died too. My neighbor insisted it was
still living as if insisting could make it
bloom again. His parents were still
alive so I let him believe. One morning,
small black sprinklers in the pot. I had
forgotten about the hope of others. I
had forgotten about others. I only had
one friend left—Death. That year, I quit
my job. When I brushed my children's
hair, birds flew out from underneath.
My mother would not have approved. I
can see her face as I tell her the wrong
story. As time passes, my memories
of her are like a night animal racing
across the roof. I know it is an animal,
but I will never be able to see it or know
when it will come again.

Similes—died on August 3, 2015. There was nothing like death, just death. Nothing like grief, just grief. How the shadow of a chain-link fence can look like a fish's scales but never be. Once my mother called late at night because she was constipated. The streetlamps still looked like things with their long arched arms. I sat on her bed in the dark. The glow from the bathroom light still like everything. I filled and emptied the plastic sitz bath that looked like something. Her two elbows still able to make small bowls on her knees. I gave her instructions and said nothing more. If only words could represent thought in the way a microphone represents words.

Affection—died on November 12, 1978, the last picture I see of my mother's arms around me. At the funeral, I never touched my sister. When the room was finally empty, she sat in the front row with her spouse. I watched his arm lift and fall onto her shoulder. When my spouse's parents died, both times, he burst into tears, inextinguishable tears that quickly extinguished. The first time, he hugged me and not his family. The second time, he hugged no one. When the nurse called, she said, *I'm sorry, but your mother passed away this morning.* When I told my children, the three of us hugged in a circle, burst *into* tears. As if the tears were already there crying on their own and we, the newly bereaved, exploded into them. In the returning out of the tears, the first person *I* dissolves a little more each time.

Home—died sometime around 1960 when my mother left Taiwan. Home died again on August 3, 2015. Home's fingertips trimmed off each time. New stubs became conscious, became heads of state, just shorter and fatter. Now home is a looking glass called Rose Hills Memorial Park. How far she has traveled from Beijing to Taiwan to New York to Pennsylvania to Michigan to California to Rose Hills. When a white writer has a character call another a *squinty-eyed cunt,* I search for my mother. I call her name but I can't remember her voice. I think it is squinty. She would have said, *Don't listen to lao mei, we all end up in the same place.* But where is that place? Are there doors there? Cattails? Now there are barbed wires in her throat, her words are stillbirth. All the new flat tombstones since my last visit, little stretchers on the lawn. I lie down next to her stone, close my eyes. I know many things now. Even with my eyes closed, I know a bird passes over me. In hangman, the body forms while it is being hung. As in, we grow as we are dying.

When a mother dies,
a house becomes a forest.
My children, children,
know that I am in the trees.
True love means you won't find me.

*

My children, children,
remember to let me go,
delete my number,
save the number of the trees.
Remember, the lemons speak.

The Bees—268 million years old from the Philippines, passed away on April 26, 2217 in Nome, Alaska. The detaching icebergs crushed the bees who used to fly over conference rooms. Once I nearly died in a small plane with a CEO, CFO, and COO during their IPO. On the ground, the CEO glared at me, as if I had caused the storm. As if the yellow lights had come from my mind. As if the buzzing had come from my shaking. As if the lightning were a box I had tripped over. Maybe he was right. Maybe I had become estranged from a part of myself that wanted to stay alive. That wanted them to remain alive. In the same way I had become estranged from my mother forever, but not from her death.

Victoria Chang—died on August 3, 2015, the one who never used to weep when other people's parents died. Now I ask questions, I bring glasses. I shake the trees in my dreams so I can tremble with others tomorrow. Only one of six siblings came to the funeral, the oldest uncle. A few called and cried or asked questions. This uncle said he knew something had happened because the morning my mother died he felt someone kick him, certain it was her. Now I know others found my mother difficult too. But she was not his mother. She was mine, all mine. Therefore anger toward her was mine. All mine. Anger after someone has died is a cake on a table, fully risen. A knife housed in glass.

Clothes—died on August 10, 2015. We stuffed them into lawn bags to donate. Shirt after shirt, button-down after button-down, dress after dress, limb after limb. A few leapt out to me like the flame from a nightmare, the kind of flame that almost seems human in its gestures. I kept those. I kept the hundreds of pencils. I am writing with a pencil from my mother's drawer. It says *Detroit Public Schools,* where she taught. Each sentence fights me. Once we rolled her downstairs, played croquet and putt-putt golf. She sat and watched, her vacant eyes not seeing anything we saw. As if she were looking beyond us, beyond the sun. The days of August already made a certain way that she could see and we couldn't. I left her in the sun too long. One child doing cartwheels on the grass as my mother looked on, wearing the white blouse with the small pink flowers swirling in a pattern. I kept the stare. I kept the flowers. And I donated the vacant shirt.

Guilt—never died on August 3, 2017. I hired a hit man to use a missile. But guilt still lies in a heap on my chest at night like a pile of frozen pigeons. Last month, my father fell again and I walked through him for the third time. They told me he was trying to run away and tripped. Another brain bleed. We moved him upstairs to memory care, as if strangers could somehow care for his memory. When I visited, no one could find him. We opened one door after another, the square-tipped smells of each person rushed out. We found him in someone else's bed, hair buzzing. He handed me his glasses and said, *Here's my future.* And all I could think was, *What would my dead mother do?* I went from room to room looking for her. All I found were dismembered shadows and bodies in C shapes, heads emptied out. I could hear all of the hearts beating in the dark. The problem was they all sounded the same. My own heart slowed. Guilt had turned into a heart too, mixed in the pile, breeding with all the other hearts.

The Ocean—died on August 21, 2017, when I didn't jump from the ship. Instead, I dragged the door shut and pulled up the safety latch. The water in my body wanted to pour into the ocean and I imagined myself being washed by the water, my body separating into the droplets it always was. I could feel the salt on my neck for days. A woman I once knew leapt out of a window to her death. The difference was she was being chased. Some scientists say the ocean is warming. Some say the ocean has hypoxic areas with no oxygen. Even water has hierarchy. A child's death is worse than a woman's death unless the woman who died was the mother of the child and the only parent. If the woman who died was the mother of an adult, it is merely *a part of life.* If both mother and daughter die together, it is *a shame.* If a whole family dies, it is *a catastrophe.* What will we call a whole ocean's death? *Peace.*

The Face—died on August 3, 2015, along with the body, particles of gray dust and small white bones. The face represents a personhood, the part we show to others the most. Could I identify my mother by her hands? Her feet? On the way to JFK, an old cemetery, headstones all different sizes, tilted. The headstone represents a person's face, not in the same way a photo represents a face. A horn means something. It makes us look up and out at the train. When the train leaves, the tracks represent an absence but also imply a train once existed. Imply a hope, a return. Maybe there are no beginnings. Maybe nothing is an elegy, in the way rain from indoors is neither a beginning nor an end.

My children say *no,*
I say *yes* because I know.
I tell them they can.
But today, people were shot.
We walk into a blender.

*

Have you ever looked
so closely at a child's face
that you could see God,
see the small hairs that you know
will lift with each new shooting?

IV

The canopy of civilisation is burnt out. The sky is dark as polished whale-bone. But there is a kindling in the sky whether of lamplight or of dawn. There is a stir of some sort— sparrows on plane trees somewhere chirping.

—Virginia Woolf, *The Waves*

America—died on February 14, 2018, and my dead mother doesn't know. Since her death, America has died a series of small deaths, each one less precise than the next. My tears are now shaped like hooks but my heart is damp still. If it is lucky, it is in the middle of its beats. The unlucky dead children hold telegrams they must hand to a woman at a desk. The woman will collect their belongings and shadows. My dead mother asks each of these children if they know me, have seen me, how tall my children are now. They will tell her that they once lived in Florida, not California. She will see the child with the hole in his head. She will blow the dreams out of the hole like dust. I used to think death was a kind of anesthesia. Now I imagine long lines, my mother taking in all the children. I imagine her touching their hair. How she might tickle their knees to make them laugh. The dead hold the other half of our ticket. The dead are an image of wind. And when they comb their hair, our trees rustle.

I am ready to
admit I love my children.
To admit this is
to admit that they will die.
Die: no one knows this but words.

*

My children, children,
this poem will not end because
I am trying to
end this poem with hope hope hope,
see how the mouth stays open?

Notes

During the process of writing the *Obit* poems, I referenced
Virginia Woolf's *The Waves* and plucked out occasional
words to spark my imagination.

Only after I had written "My Mother's Lungs" did I read
Blue Nights by Joan Didion and find that she had a similar
thought about time change and death.

"I am a miner. The light burns blue." is the first line of Sylvia
Plath's poem "Nick and the Candlestick."

The phrase "Imagination is having to live in a dead person's
future" in the poem "The Blue Dress" is inspired by Richard
Siken's line "I live in someone else's future" from his book
War of the Foxes.

The phrase "in the way rain from indoors is neither a
beginning nor an end" in the poem "The Face" is inspired
by Brian Teare's line "the way from indoors the sound of rain
is both figure and ground" from his book *The Empty Form
Goes All the Way to Heaven.*

Acknowledgments

Thank you to the editors of the following journals in which many of the poems in this book appeared, often in earlier forms:

The Academy of American Poets Poem-a-Day: "The Blue Dress" and "My Father's Frontal Lobe"

Adroit Journal: "My Mother's Favorite Potted Tree," "Similes," and "Tomas Tranströmer"

AGNI: "Control" and "Optimism—died of monotony"

Alaska Quarterly Review: "Hindsight" and "Reason"

The American Poetry Review: "Empathy," "Language—It wanted to live," and "Time"

At Length: "Doctors—Dr. Lynch was supposed to," "Friendships—died a slow death," "Home—died sometime around 1960," "Memory—It was a routine" (as "Money"), "Subject Matter," and "Yesterday"

Blackbird: "Hope" "Victoria Chang—died unknowingly," and "Voice Mail"

The Georgia Review: "Approval" "Language—died again," "The Priest," and "Victoria Chang—the one who never used to weep"

Guernica: "The Future"

Kenyon Review: "Affection" "The Clock," "Clothes," "Friendships—died once beloved," "The Ocean," and "Optimism—died a slow death into a pavement"

Michigan Quarterly Review: "Appetite—Once, in graduate school," "Form—my children sleep," "Hands," "Memory—When I returned," and "Secrets"

Mississippi Review: "Privacy" and "Tears"

Narrative: "Appetite—died its final death," "Doctors—Dr. Lynch, Dr. Chang, Dr. Mahoney," "My Mother," "Oxygen," "The Situation," and "Tankas," published together as a group

New England Review: "Grief," "Memory—The death was not sudden," and "Music"

The Normal School: "The Head—died on August 3" and "Home—died on January 12, 2013"

Ploughshares: "Civility" and "Logic"

Poetry: "Caretakers" and "My Mother's Teeth"

Poetry London: "Victoria Chang—died unwillingly" and "The Car"

A Public Space: "The Face"

Shenandoah: "Gait" and "My Mother's Lungs"

Terrain.org: "America"

32 Poems: "The Doctors—died surrounded by" and "Obsession"

Tin House: "Form—After my mother died," "Sadness," and "Victoria Chang—died at the age of 41"

West Branch: "Ambition" and "Chair"

The Yale Review: "The Bees" and "Guilt"

Many sections of "I Am a Miner. The Light Burns Blue." were published separately in different forms in journals such as *AGNI, Blackbird, Cerise Press, Gulf Coast, Harvard Review, The Journal, Kenyon Review, Meridian, New England Review, Pleiades, The Southeast Review,* and *The Southern Review.*

"Affection," "The Clock," "Clothes," "Friendships—died once beloved," "The Ocean," and "Optimism—died a slow death into a pavement"—all poems published in the *Kenyon Review*—also appeared in *Best American Poetry 2019,* selected by Major Jackson and published by Scribner.

"Language—died, brilliant and beautiful" was anthologized in *The Eloquent Poem,* edited by Elise Paschen and published by Persea Books.

A part of this book was awarded the Poetry Society of America's 2018 Alice Fay di Castagnola Award. "The Obituary Writer" was published on PSA's website.

Thank you to Copper Canyon Press and the entire team.

Thank you to the Guggenheim Foundation, the Sustainable Arts Foundation, the Poetry Society of America, the Pushcart Prize, the Housatonic Book Awards, the Lannan Foundation, and the MacDowell Colony for support and encouragement.

Thanks to all my beloved friends and supporters—way too many to mention, but here are just a few: Ilya Kaminsky (for tirelessly reading many versions of the manuscript and for all the conversations), G.C. Waldrep + Dana Levin + John Gallaher (my trusted friends in art and life), Dean Rader, Rick Barot, David Baker, Isaac Fitzgerald, Liza Voges, Jen Chang, Maggie Smith, Ann Townsend, and Wayne Miller; my LA poet friends Van Khanna, Blas Falconer, Elline Lipkin, and

Charlie Jensen; my National Book Critics Circle colleagues; all my Antioch University colleagues (thanks Bernadette, Natalie, and Daisy!); my Idyllwild colleagues such as Ed Skoog and Heather Companiott; all my social media friends, and so many more...

Thanks to my family for tolerating my obsession with poetry and poems. Thanks to my wiener dogs, Mustard and Ketchup, for listening to me read all these poems aloud a billion times. Thank you to my father, who unknowingly has populated my poems for the last decade, and finally, thank you to my mother, whom I've never properly thanked.

About the Author

Victoria Chang's prior books are *Barbie Chang, The Boss, Salvinia Molesta,* and *Circle.* Her children's picture book, *Is Mommy?,* was illustrated by Marla Frazee and published by Beach Lane Books/Simon & Schuster. It was named a Notable Book by the *New York Times.* Her middle grade novel, *Love, Love,* was published by Sterling Publishing. She has received a Guggenheim Fellowship, a Sustainable Arts Foundation Fellowship, the Poetry Society of America's Alice Fay di Castagnola Award, a Pushcart Prize, a Lannan Residency Fellowship, and a MacDowell Colony Fellowship. She lives in Los Angeles and is the program chair of Antioch's low-residency MFA program.

Lannan Literary Selections

For two decades Lannan Foundation has supported the publication and distribution of exceptional literary works. Copper Canyon Press gratefully acknowledges their support.

LANNAN LITERARY SELECTIONS 2020

Mark Bibbins, *13th Balloon*

Victoria Chang, *Obit*

Leila Chatti, *Deluge*

Philip Metres, *Shrapnel Maps*

Natalie Shapero, *Popular Longing*

RECENT LANNAN LITERARY SELECTIONS FROM
COPPER CANYON PRESS

Sherwin Bitsui, *Dissolve*

Jericho Brown, *The Tradition*

John Freeman, *Maps*

Jenny George, *The Dream of Reason*

Ha Jin, *A Distant Center*

Deborah Landau, *Soft Targets*

Maurice Manning, *One Man's Dark*

Rachel McKibbens, *blud*

Aimee Nezhukumatathil, *Oceanic*

Camille Rankine, *Incorrect Merciful Impulses*

Paisley Rekdal, *Nightingale*

Natalie Scenters-Zapico, *Lima :: Limón*

Frank Stanford, *What About This: Collected Poems of Frank Stanford*

Ocean Vuong, *Night Sky with Exit Wounds*

C.D. Wright, *Casting Deep Shade*

Javier Zamora, *Unaccompanied*

Matthew Zapruder, *Father's Day*

Ghassan Zaqtan (translated by Fady Joudah), *The Silence That Remains*

Poetry is vital to language and living. Since 1972, Copper Canyon Press has published extraordinary poetry from around the world to engage the imaginations and intellects of readers, writers, booksellers, librarians, teachers, students, and donors.

WE ARE GRATEFUL FOR THE MAJOR SUPPORT PROVIDED BY:

THE PAUL G. ALLEN
FAMILY FOUNDATION

CULTURE

the POint
envision·enact·evolve

Anonymous
Jill Baker and Jeffrey Bishop
Anne and Geoffrey Barker
Donna and Matt Bellew
Diana Broze
John R. Cahill
The Beatrice R. and Joseph A. Coleman Foundation Inc.
The Currie Family Fund
Laurie and Oskar Eustis
Saramel and Austin Evans
Mimi Gardner Gates
Gull Industries Inc. on behalf of William True
The Trust of Warren A. Gummow
Carolyn and Robert Hedin
Bruce Kahn
Phil Kovacevich and Eric Wechsler
Lakeside Industries Inc.
on behalf of Jeanne Marie Lee
Maureen Lee and Mark Busto

TO LEARN MORE ABOUT UNDERWRITING
COPPER CANYON PRESS TITLES,
PLEASE CALL 360-385-4925 EXT. 103

WE ARE GRATEFUL FOR THE MAJOR SUPPORT PROVIDED BY:

Peter Lewis

Ellie Mathews and Carl Youngmann as The North Press

Larry Mawby

Hank Meijer

Jack Nicholson

Petunia Charitable Fund and adviser Elizabeth Hebert

Gay Phinny

Suzie Rapp and Mark Hamilton

Emily and Dan Raymond

Jill and Bill Ruckelshaus

Cynthia Sears

Kim and Jeff Seely

Dan Waggoner

Randy and Joanie Woods

Barbara and Charles Wright

Caleb Young as C. Young Creative

The dedicated interns and faithful volunteers
of Copper Canyon Press

The Chinese character for poetry is made up of two parts:
"word" and "temple." It also serves as pressmark for
Copper Canyon Press.

The poems are set in Berthold Akzidenz Grotesk.
Book design and composition by Phil Kovacevich.